THE SOUTHERN RAILWAY COLLECTION

Hampshire and Dorset Reflections

Terry Gough

· RAILWAY HERITAGE ·
from
The **NOSTALGIA** *Collection*

First published in 1984 as *The Southern in Hampshire and Dorset* by Oxford Publishing Company
New Silver Link Publishing edition first published in 2004

British Library Cataloguing in Publication Data

A catalogue record for this book is available from the British Library.

ISBN 1 85794 136 5

Silver Link Publishing Ltd
The Trundle
Ringstead Road
Great Addington
Kettering
Northants NN14 4BW

Tel/Fax: 01536 330588
email: sales@nostalgiacollection.com
Website: www.nostalgiacollection.com

Printed and bound in Great Britain

ABBREVIATIONS

BR	British Railways
DNSR	Didcot, Newbury & Southampton Railway
GNR	Great Northern Railway
GWR	Great Western Railway
LBSCR	London, Brighton & South Coast Railway
LMSR	London Midland & Scottish Railway
LSWR	London & South Western Railway
MSWJR	Midland & South Western Junction Railway
PDSWJR	Plymouth, Devonport & South Western Junction Railway
SDJR	Somerset & Dorset Joint Railway
SECR	South Eastern & Chatham Railway
SR	Southern Railway

CONTENTS

Rebuilt 'Merchant Navy' class, No. 35029, *Ellerman Lines*, is pictured with the 'up' 'Bournemouth Belle', approaching Micheldever on 12th August 1961.

INTRODUCTION

The main line through Hampshire to Southampton and beyond has the distinction of being one of the earliest main lines in the country, and the last to be steam-operated. Proposals for a railway from London to Southampton were first made in 1825, but it was not until 1840 that such a line was completed. It was extremely well engineered, and ran from Nine Elms through the small townships of South-East London to Woking, and thence on to Basingstoke and Winchester. It is remarkable that the line climbed almost imperceptibly, virtually from the moment it crossed into Hampshire, to a summit just west of Basingstoke. It then descended the whole length of the journey to Southampton. There were no sharp curves, thus the line was ideally suited to fast running.

The railway was built with the major objective of capturing trade from the port of Southampton. Originally known as the London & Southampton Railway, it changed its name to the London & South Western Railway (LSWR) in 1839. It was so successful that additional intermediate stations were added in the succeeding years. The LSWR was also extending its territory westwards to Salisbury, and had built another main line connecting London with Portsmouth. Southampton itself was expanding, both in terms of population and commercially, and in 1892 the LSWR took over ownership of the docks. In the early 1900s, much of the route to Southampton was widened to provide two 'up' and two 'down' lines. The Southampton & Dorchester Railway, known colloquially as 'Castleman's Corkscrew', after the name of the promoter and the geometry of the line respectively, was also part of the LSWR system. The LSWR built numerous secondary and branch lines, some to capture potential traffic which never materialized, some to keep competing railway companies at bay and others actually for the benefit of the local community. In the first category, the most famous is probably the line through the Meon Valley, which was built as a through route for Isle of Wight traffic. It was eclipsed by the LSWR's own more direct line to Portsmouth, and slowly fell into obscurity. Lines from Andover and Hurstbourne were built mainly as a means of preventing other companies pushing their way towards Southampton. Lines such as those between Southampton and Portsmouth, and the Lymington branch were, at least, in part of local benefit, and are still performing that function today.

'King Arthur' class, No. 30790 *Sir Villiars* approaches Brockenhurst, with the 6.35p.m. Bournemouth West to Reading General service, on 7th June 1960.

Some of the development of the railway system occurred in a rather piecemeal manner, particularly in the Bournemouth area, resulting in considerable duplication of effort. However, by the turn of the century the railways of Hampshire were virtually complete. It was not until 1925 that the Southern Railway added to the system, by constructing a line along the western edge of Southampton Water to Fawley, although in the intervening period some minor lines had been closed. The railways of Hampshire contracted a little in the 1930s, when several branch lines lost their passenger services. Amongst these were Hurstbourne to Fullerton Junction and Botley to Bishop's Waltham. The next change had far-reaching effects on the prosperity of the railway, and indeed on the places it served. This was the Southern Railway's electrification programme of the late 1930s, and included two of the lines radiating into Hampshire from Woking. These were the main line to Portsmouth and the line through Farnham to Alton. The immediate effect was to change the pattern of travel, which had been so well established. On the main line, the express electric trains, which stopped at three intermediate stations, covered the journey to Portsmouth in the same time as the former non-stop steam trains. Although Alton also benefited, the electrification was detrimental to the lines beyond Alton, which no longer enjoyed through trains from London, and they eventually closed. The electrification also resulted in the first major displacement of the steam engine from Hampshire, a pattern repeated on two further occasions in the history of the county.

The late Southern Railway period provided excellent main-line services to Bournemouth and into Dorset, with the introduction of Bulleid Light Pacifics and modern rolling stock. After nationalization, the main line had recovered from the effects of war, but other lines had suffered badly and were in a run-down condition, and relied upon pre-Grouping motive power and rolling stock. Services were often sparse, even in areas of high population density. The potential traffic, which could be generated by the provision of a frequent integrated fixed interval service throughout southern Hampshire, was realized by British Railways, and a programme of modernization was launched. All secondary services were to be operated by diesel multiple units, and apart from main line and certain cross-country trains, steam was to be virtually eliminated from passenger trains. The diesel units were built at Eastleigh, and the first entered service in September 1957 on the Portsmouth to Salisbury via Southampton and Southampton to Winchester lines. In November of the same year, steam was ousted from both the Portsmouth to Andover via Eastleigh, and Southampton to Alton lines. The frequency of services was hourly on most lines, where sometimes in the past there had been gaps of three hours. Between Southampton and Winchester, the interval was half-hourly, almost unknown anywhere outside the London suburban area. The scheme was an immediate commercial success, and to the Southern Region's embarrassment the two car units were frequently overcrowded. Plans were drawn up for the building of trailer coaches, although these were not available for some time, prior to which the units were often operated in pairs at peak times. Further proposed stages in the modernization programme included services from Portsmouth to Basingstoke and Reading, from Salisbury to Bournemouth West, Brockenhurst to Bournemouth West via Ringwood, and even the 'all stations' service on the main line from Southampton to Weymouth. In the event, only the former route became diesel unit-operated, the two lines to Bournemouth West retaining steam traction until their closure. Diesel multiple unit services were also proposed for the branch lines to Lymington, Swanage and, most interesting of all, Gosport, which had been closed to passengers since 1953. Lymington and Swanage were both dieselized, but this only lasted a very short time before the former line was electrified and the latter closed.

The Southern Region also turned its attention to the future of the

main line, and gave serious consideration to the use of a 25kV overhead electric system from Waterloo to Weymouth. This was still under consideration in 1963, although later the same year the decision was taken to extend the existing third rail system from the Woking area. The intention was that all trains would be locomotive-hauled, but these plans were changed by the later decision not to electrify beyond Bournemouth. It was then announced that electric multiple units, coupled to a non-powered unit, would be used between London and Bournemouth, and would be push-pull operated. At Bournemouth the non-powered unit alone would be taken on to Weymouth, with a diesel locomotive. Boat-trains, other special passenger trains and freight trains would be in the hands of electro-diesel locomotives, which had been introduced in Kent for its electrification programme. The advantage of this dual form of traction was that it avoided the necessity to lay conductor rails in sidings. It also eliminated the need to change locomotives at the extremities of the electrified system. The electro-diesel locomotives for Hampshire were built in 1965. The electric multiple units consisted mainly of British Railways steam stock, notably from the Midland Region, which were rebuilt for the Southern Region at York and Eastleigh. Thus of necessity the motor coaches, which were new, had bodies of classical BR design. No advantage was taken of improvements which were incorporated into the BR Mk. II coaches, built at about the same time for locomotive-hauled trains on other regions.

The electric service was introduced as far as Basingstoke at the beginning of 1967, and by the spring most trains were formed of electric units, although they ran to steam schedules. The full service began officially on 10th July 1967, and included an hourly fast train stopping only at Southampton. The journey time was 1 hour 40 minutes, compared with 2 hours by steam.

The Alton to Winchester line, diesel-operated for the previous ten years, was also considered for electrification in 1967. Unfortunately, not only was the idea abandoned, but so was the line itself. It was subsequently closed to all traffic, thus depriving the region of its long established alternative route between London and Winchester. It also resulted in loss of local and commuting traffic, although part of the line is now privately operated.

The years 1957 and 1967 were thus of great importance in the development of railways in Hampshire. In both years, the travelling public saw significant improvements in services. For the railway enthusiast, the first occasion resulted in the demise of steam on secondary services. Ten years later, the electrification of the Bournemouth line saw complete elimination of steam engines from Hampshire and Dorset. This book is a photographic record of the steam services during that decade. A small number of changes have been made since the first edition. Changes have also taken place on the railways, most notably electrification of more lines, including Weymouth.

Terry Gough
Sherbourne
2004

Author's Note

All stations mentioned in the text are included on the accompanying map, which shows the railways as at 1957. Completely closed railways are marked as dotted lines.

Steam services on lines in Hampshire and Dorset are also covered in several of my other books.

Specifically excluded from this book is the Lyme Regis branch, which although partly in Dorset, is covered in *Southern Reflections: The West Country* in this series. British Rail is thanked for the provision of a lineside pass.

DORSET & HAMPSHIRE

SCALE

4 Miles

N

To Woking
To Ascot
To Reading
Ash Vale
To Guildford
Farnborough
To Reading
To Guildford
Alton
Farringdon
Basingstoke
To Reading
Medstead & Four Marks
Ropley
Alresford
Micheldever
To Newbury
Whitchurch North
Chesil
Shawford
Winchester City
To Brighton
Havant
Langston
Hayling Island
Fratton
Southsea
Knowle
Botley
Bishop's Waltham
Fareham
Gosport
Portsmouth Harbour
Bursledon
Eastleigh
St. Denys
Southampton Terminus
Southampton Central
Fawley
Redbridge
Millbrook
Marchwood
Hurstbourne
Andover
Fullerton
Mottisfont
Dunbridge
Romsey
Totton
Lyndhurst Road
Beaulieu Road
Brockenhurst
Lymington Town
Lymington Pier
Grateley
To Cheltenham
To Salisbury
Dean
Braemore
To Salisbury
Ringwood
Holmsley
Sway
Christchurch
Bournemouth Central
Bournemouth West
West Moors
Wimborne
Poole
To Bath
Broadstone
Hamworthy Jcn.
Wareham
Corfe Castle
Swanage
Wool
Dorchester South
To Yeovil
Weymouth

FARNBOROUGH TO BASINGSTOKE

Plate 1: The Southern main line, to Bournemouth and the West of England, enters Hampshire from Surrey in style, with four tracks consisting of 'down' local and 'down' through lines, and the two corresponding 'up' lines. The county boundary is the course of the Blackwater River, which runs in a northerly direction, and is little more than a stream at its intersection with the railway. The SECR line from Guildford to Reading follows the river for many miles, and also passes under the ex-LSWR main line at this point. On 26th March 1964, Class 5MT BR Standard 4-6-0 locomotive, No. 73046, crosses the county boundary, with the 1.54p.m. Waterloo to Basingstoke semi-fast train.

Plate 2: Summer Saturday mornings saw a number of empty carriage workings from Basingstoke to Waterloo, for 'down' holiday expresses operating later in the day. Here, Class S15, No. 30833 is seen hauling empty stock through the cutting east of Farnborough, during August 1964.

Plate 3: A 'down' express freight train destined for Southampton, is pictured on the through line near the site of Sturt Lane Junction, east of Farnborough, on 26th March 1964. The engine is Class S15, No. 30838, and of particular interest are the conductor rails on the outer lines. All four lines were electrified from Waterloo as far as Woking, but beyond there, only the local 'up' and 'down' lines for Alton and Ascot were electrified. The Alton line left the main line at Pirbright Junction, between Brookwood and Farnborough. The third rail continued beyond Pirbright to Sturt Lane Junction, where two spurs ran to Frimley Junction, thus connecting the main line from the east and west with the Ash Vale to Ascot line. The west spur was closed to passengers in 1937, but the east spur, which was electrified in 1939, had a passenger service running from Woking to Ascot. The east spur lasted until well after nationalization, but both spurs have now been taken up.

Plate 4: Departing from Farnborough, on 15th October 1960, is Class 5MT, No. 73118 on the 12.12p.m. stopping train from Basingstoke to Waterloo. This is one of a batch of ten engines of this class, built at Doncaster in 1955 for the Southern Region. After withdrawal of the ex-LSWR 'King Arthur' class engines, their names were given to these Standard locomotives, No. 73118 being named *King Leodegrance*. In the background is a gantry of LSWR lower quadrant signals. On the section of main line between Brookwood and Grateley, some 25 miles beyond Basingstoke, on the West of England main line, all signals were pneumatically operated. This was an experiment initiated by the LSWR *(see Plate 21)*, and the system was installed on this section of the line in 1904. Although not extended to any other part of the railway network, it remained in use until the introduction of colour light signals in 1966. It was an eerie experience to be on the lineside, particularly in misty weather, as the pneumatics continually emitted odd hissing sounds where the system leaked, and when signals were set.

Plate 5: Class S15, No. 30833 again, with a 'down' freight train runs, more conventionally, on the local line at Farnborough, on 15th October 1960. The S15 locomotives were introduced by Urie for heavy goods work, but were based on the 'King Arthur' express passenger design. The first batch of ten S15 locomotives was built in 1920/1, and further batches were built between 1926 and 1936, these differing in detail both visually and internally. All of these engines were built at Eastleigh Works and there was a total of forty five engines in the class. They all lasted until 1962 when withdrawals began, and several have since been preserved, including one for eventual static display at Eastleigh.

Plate 6: A 'down' express, bound for the West of England, approaches Farnborough. The engine is 'Lord Nelson' class, No. 30853 *Sir Richard Grenville*, and the train is the 10.54a.m. Waterloo to Salisbury, pictured on 15th October 1960. The stock is a Bournemouth dining set, No. 299. The 'Lord Nelson' class was built by the Southern Railway between 1926 and 1929, the first engine, No. 850, taking the name of the class. They were built for the Waterloo expresses and the Eastern Section continental trains, although after nationalization, they spent most of their time on the Salisbury and Bournemouth trains. The 10.54a.m. service called at Surbiton, Woking and then all stations to Salisbury; rather a lowly duty for such an engine. The first of the class was withdrawn in 1961 and by the end of the following year, all sixteen had been withdrawn. However, *Lord Nelson* itself was destined for preservation, and although it remained in store for many years, it is now back in use and may be seen working special trains on Britain's railways.

Plate 7: Stopping trains, between Basingstoke and Waterloo, were hauled by a variety of locomotives, usually provided by Basingstoke or Nine Elms sheds. On this occasion, the 11.10a.m. from Basingstoke was graced by a well-kept rebuilt 'West Country' class, No. 34046 *Braunton*, an easy task for such a powerful machine. All stopping trains between Basingstoke and Woking had to use the local line, because there were no platforms serving the centre roads. The author knows of one occasion when this fact was forgotten by the Woking signalman, who dispatched an evening rush-hour train to Basingstoke on the through line. Its first scheduled stop out of Woking was Brookwood, which it passed at a sedate 0 m.p.h. much to the distress of those on board. The remains of the centre platform, seen in this photograph, was the original 'down' platform, in use prior to the quadrupling of the line from Woking to Worting Junction in 1904. The two new lines were for 'down' trains, and the original 'down' line, seen in the foreground, became the 'up' through line. At the same time, the station was rebuilt and a new 'down' platform was provided.

Plate 8: On 15th October 1960, another 'Lord Nelson' class, No. 30857 *Lord Howe*, heads a train which is more in keeping with its status and capability. This is the 11.30a.m. Waterloo to Bournemouth express with a first stop at Basingstoke, 57 minutes after leaving Waterloo. To Bournemouth, there was an hourly express service, the 12.30p.m. being the 'Bournemouth Belle'. On alternate hours, there were through coaches running on to Weymouth. The pattern was not strictly at fixed intervals, and the number of intermediate calls also varied. The siding and platform on the right was for troop trains. The signal box, between the running lines and this siding, was built at the time of the widening, and was closed in 1966. From Farnborough, there was a short branch into the Royal Aircraft Establishment, whose property included an ex-SECR six-wheeled brake van, now preserved on the Kent & East Sussex Railway.

Plate 9 (left upper): Despite being freight engines, Class S15 locomotives were often called upon to work semi-fast passenger trains, particularly in the summer months and after most of the 'King Arthur' class locomotives had been withdrawn. Entering Basingstoke, on 12th September 1964, is No. 30839 with the 12.39p.m. service from Waterloo; a slow train with a journey time of one hour sixteen minutes. On the right are the carriage sidings, with a rebuilt 'Merchant Navy' class locomotive waiting to leave. In 1848, the GWR broad gauge from Reading reached Basingstoke, and a junction with the LSWR was installed twelve years later when the GWR became mixed gauge. The line to Reading is still open, and has a regular passenger service. It is also a vital link for inter-regional through trains.

Plate 11: The 1.24p.m. (SO) Waterloo to Salisbury train, is seen in Basingstoke Cutting, just east of the station, on 12th September 1964. The train was the 'all stations' from Woking service. From Monday to Friday, the train started from Basingstoke, with a connection from the 1.30p.m. Waterloo to Bournemouth fast train. The engine is rebuilt 'Battle of Britain' class, No. 34059 *Sir Archibald Sinclair*. These engines were identical to the 'West Country' class in all respects, other than name, whether in original or rebuilt condition.

Plate 12: A special train of Pullman coaches, run in connection with the Farnborough Air Show, leaves Basingstoke behind rebuilt 'West Country' class, No. 34037 *Clovelly*, on 12th September 1964. The first vehicle was built by the Metropolitan Carriage & Wagon Co. in 1928, whereas all the other Pullman coaches are post-war vehicles. Pullman stock was regularly seen passing through Basingstoke on the 'Bournemouth Belle', and for the short period between 1947 and 1954, on the 'Devon Belle'. It was also sometimes used on Waterloo to Southampton Docks boat trains.

Plate 10 (left lower): During August 1965, BR Standrd Class 4MT, No. 76031, is approaching Basingstoke with a 'down' freight train. Electrification of the main line through to Bournemouth was well advanced by this time, and the third rail had been laid as far as Basingstoke on both the 'up' and 'down' local lines. Most of the pre-war Southern motive power and rolling stock had been withdrawn, and in the background some condemned coaches can be seen. Despite the closed signal box, semaphore signals were still in operation. The new power box at Basingstoke did not come into operation until the following year.

Plate 13 (below): The beginning of the journey for Class S15, No. 30509, with the 3.12p.m. 'all stations' to Woking train. This was an unusual service, in that unlike other trains, it did not continue to Waterloo. The engine is one of the first batch of S15 locomotives, and comparison with *Plate 9* clearly shows them to have a somewhat older, but nevertheless attractive, appearance. The train is standing in platform 4 of the five platforms at Basingstoke, with platforms 2 and 3 being the centre island. Platform 5 was for the Reading General trains, and was part of the original GWR terminus which, until 1932, was operated as a separate station.

Plate 14 (right upper): Basingstoke Shed was situated on the 'up' side of the main line, at the Salisbury end of the station. It provided motive power for most of the slow and semi-fast trains to London and Salisbury, and also for some of the Bournemouth services. It had an allocation of about twenty locomotives. Until the advent of BR Standard tender engines, these consisted predominantly of Southern Railway Moguls, together with 'King Arthurs' and 4-4-0s and a few ageing Drummond 700 class engines used for freight operations. It was also common to see 'West Country' and 'Schools' class locomotives, along with other visitors from major Western Section sheds, including Nine Elms. On 25th August 1962, Class S15, No. 30514 from Feltham is seen on Basingstoke Shed together with an LSWR 700 class engine, No. 30368, which had been allocated to Basingstoke, at least since nationalization.

Plate 15 (right lower): One of the last of the 'King Arthur' class locomotives to operate the semi-fast trains to Waterloo was No. 30777 *Sir Lamiel*, seen on shed on 22nd May 1960. In the background, a 'West Country' Pacific is just visible. The 'King Arthur' class locomotives were introduced by the LSWR in 1917 and, despite early misgivings, evolved as an extremely successful design, giving main line service long after the introduction of the Bulleid Pacifics. The photograph shows one of the later batch of thirty 'King Arthurs' which were introduced by the Southern Railway, but built by the North British Locomotive Co. in 1925. The Southern Railway itself built twenty four of these engines at Eastleigh, making a total, with the original engines, of seventy four.

Plate 16: Two Class G6 locomotives [ ] been allocated to Basingstoke for many ye[ ] for station pilot duties. No. 30258 is seen [ ] of service, under the shear legs, on 22nd M[ ] 1960. It was withdrawn the following ye[ ] These engines were built by Adams at N[ ] Elms Works, from 1894, for shunting du[ ] and use on local goods trains. They were v[ ] similar in appearance to the Class 02 0-[ ] tank engines *(see Plate 57).* Although furt[ ] Class G6 locomotives were built under [ ] Drummond regime, they were somew[ ] different from the first batch.

Plate 17: Several 4-6-0 engines can be se[ ] near the coaling stage at Basingstoke on 3[ ] August 1961, the engine in the foregrou[ ] being 'King Arthur' class No. 30773 [ ] *Lavaine.* Basingstoke Shed was closed w[ ] the passing of steam, and was demolished [ ] 1969.

Plate 18: In Basingstoke's 'up' West Yard, on 10th September 1959, a ballast train from Meldon has just arrived. Meldon is situated a few miles west of Okehampton, and the quarries provided ballast for the whole of the Southern Region. The engine is Class S15, No. 30824 from Salisbury Shed. The ballast wagons, although of Southern Railway design, are known as 'Walruses', following the former GWR practice of naming wagons after amphibious and other creatures.

Plate 19: The line to Bournemouth diverged at Worting Junction the two centre lines being for the West Country. Just beyond the junction was Battledown Flyover, which enabled 'up' Bournemouth trains to join the West of England line without obstructing the 'down' lines. Beyond Worting, the respective main lines were double track. Battledown Flyover was a favourite place for photographers, but it needed careful timing to photograph more than one train simultaneously from the lineside. This photograph, taken on 7th June 1960, was the result of my good fortune and was taken from the window of a Reading General to Portsmouth & Southsea train, which was running late. The 'Battle of Britain' class locomotive, No. 34052 *Lord Dowding*, pictured with an Exeter train, had left Waterloo at 9.00a.m. The two trains were scheduled to leave Basingstoke at 9.53a.m. and 10.05a.m. respectively. The 'up' train from Salisbury, hauled by 'King Arthur' class, No. 30799 *Sir Ironside*, was due at Basingstoke at 9.48a.m., and was running late, all of which resulted in coincident arrival at Battledown.

Plate 20: The 7.20a.m. Waterloo to Salisbury train is pictured at Whitchurch North on 13th August 1964, with Standard Class 5MT, No. 73088 *Joyous Gard*, which was built at Derby *(see Plate 4)*. Until 1949 the station was named Whitchurch and in 1972 it was changed again from Whitchurch North to Whitchurch (Hants). There was also a second station at Whitchurch, on the Didcot, Newbury & Southampton line of the GWR, thus giving the inhabitants of Whitchurch both east-west and north-south services. The Didcot, Newbury & Southampton Railway's station later became known as Whitchurch Town, reflecting its better siting than that of the LSWR station, and there were plans to link the DNSR to the LSWR main line at both Whitchurch and Micheldever *(see Plate 23)*. These plans were abandoned and, in the event, the connection was made south of Winchester at Shawford Junction *(see Plate 30)*. In 1960 the Newbury to Southampton service was withdrawn, but the Southern Region station still has a two hourly service, with additional trains in the morning and evening.

Plate 21: The same train as that seen in the previous photograph leaves Grateley on Salisbury Plain. Although by now very forlorn, it was the junction station for a branch to Amesbury, which was opened in 1901 for military traffic. The branch itself left the main line three miles from Grateley, in the Salisbury direction. In 1904, an extra line running parallel to the main line was added, to enable independent operation of the branch trains. At the same time, a connection was added to give access to the branch from the west, and subsequently the regular passenger service ran from Salisbury. Grateley itself was the railhead for both freight and troop trains for the branch, with sidings seen on the left of the photograph. The branch was extended beyond Amesbury to Bulford in 1906, but was cut back to Amesbury in 1952 when the whole line was closed to passengers. The freight only service to Amesbury was withdrawn in 1963. It was at Grateley that the first pneumatic signalling in the United Kingdom was installed in 1901 *(see Plate 4)*. The West of England line crosses the county boundary into Wiltshire, just beyond Grateley.

Plate 22: A Nine Elms to Southampton Docks freight train, viewed from the approach to Battledown Flyover, on 12th April 1962. The engine, Class S15, No. 30833, is making rather heavy weather of the load, particularly as the line is level at this point and even out of Basingstoke, the gradient is only 1 in 249. The Southern Railway had always indulged in a game of 'musical chairs' where locomotives and tenders were concerned. The locomotive in this photograph has a 4,000 gallon six-wheeled tender, but when built, No. 833, had a 5,000 gallon six-wheeled tender, although these were not fitted to all locomotives of this batch. However, this particular tender was transferred to a 'Lord Nelson' class locomotive in 1928, and replaced by a similar tender from a 'King Arthur'. A few years later, No. 833 was given a smaller tender, and the tradition was continued by BR, who presented No. 30833 with a 'Schools' tender, a few weeks after this photograph was taken. Some Class S15 locomotives were fitted with bogie tenders *(see Plate 14)*.

Plate 23: The first station beyond Worting Junction on the Bournemouth line is Micheldever. It was, at first, optimistically called Andover Road, although Andover was ten miles away to the west. However, with the opening of the line to Salisbury, and the fact that a station to serve Andover was located on the edge of the town, the name Micheldever was adopted. On summer Saturdays, this stretch of line was busy, not only with the Waterloo to Bournemouth trains, but also with through trains from other regions. These reached the Southern Region via the Reading to Basingstoke line. Passing Micheldever, on 12th August 1961, with a train of Southern Railway stock, is BR Standard Class 4MT, No. 75079 of Basingstoke Shed, with the 9.20a.m. Birkenhead to Bournemouth West service.

Plate 24: A quieter day at Micheldever, on 16th September 1959. The local freight train has just arrived in the hands of Class S15 No. 304961 and is being studied by the shunter and a porter. The station buildings, which include accommodation for the station master, are typical of the larger LSWR stations throughout Hampshire. Micheldever itself was little more than a village, and the anticipated growth of traffic did not materialize. When the lines through the station were quadrupled in 1904, the 'down' platform became a disused island as at Farnborough *(see Plate 7)*. However, in 1966, two of the lines were taken out, and the abandoned platform was rebuilt to serve all 'up' and 'down' trains.

Plate 25: Between Worting Junction and Micheldever, the railway passes under the chalk downs through three tunnels, the last of which is within sight of the station. 'West Country' class locomotive No. 34102 *Lapford* has just emerged from this tunnel with the 4.20p.m. Waterloo to Bournemouth West train in August 1961. Micheldever was used for many years as a dumping ground for rolling stock awaiting repair at Eastleigh Carriage & Wagon Works. Condemned stock was also stored here, and in the background can be seen many of the Southern Railway bogie parcels vans, known as corridor PMVs. These were built in 1930/1 on old LSWR underframes, and still retained their original bogies. They were used mostly on the Western Section for newspaper traffic, and were often attached to passenger trains. Most were cut up later in 1961 but a few passed into departmental use, and at least one was still in existence in 1983. There was also an oil storage depot at Micheldever, which was installed during World War II.

Plate 26: Another summer Saturday working was the 8.30a.m. Newcastle to Bournemouth West train, on this occasion portraying an unusual combination of a GWR 'Modified Hall', No. 7911 *Lady Margaret Hall*, a Thompson TK vehicle, and BR Standard coaches. Despite being on the Southern Region, where the engine headcodes signify the route, the visiting engine is displaying the train classification code used on all other regions, in this case that of an express passenger train.

Plate 27: Most of the London to Bournemouth expresses stopped at Winchester, which was known after nationalization as Winchester City, to distinguish it from Winchester (Chesil) on the Didcot, Newbury & Southampton Railway line. It reverted to Winchester upon the introduction of the electric services in 1967. A Class B4 0-4-0 tank engine was used as station pilot, and would often attach or detach parcels vans to and from the London trains. On 30th August 1961, this task was being performed by No. 30096, which is dwarfed even by the adjacent van. By contrast, the train engine is a 'West Country' Pacific.

Plate 28 (left upper):   Two years later, the same Class B4 engine is still on duty at Winchester. The B4 locomotives were introduced in 1891 by Adams as dock shunting engines, with twenty being built at Nine Elms. A further five were built in 1908 by Drummond. The latter were known for a short while as Class K14, and were the last engines to be built at Nine Elms. The Drummond engines were readily distinguishable as their domes were situated further from the smokebox than on the Adams engines. Over the years, their boilers were interchanged, so the difference was no longer a reliable guide to their origin. The Adams engines were built with stovepipe chimneys, but these were gradually replaced by more attractive lipped chimneys. Some engines had cutaway cabs, but these were filled in during Southern Railway ownership. Even after conversion they were easily identifiable, as they retained their centre window, in addition to two new windows *(see Plate 27)*. Most of the B4 locomotives were named, with No. 30096 being *Normandy*. Following the arrival of the USA tank engines for Southampton Docks *(see Plate 77)*, several of the B4 locomotives were sold, but twelve were retained by British Railways. The numbers were further reduced by withdrawals over the succeeding years, and by 1963, there were only three left. No. 30096 was sold to a coal merchant in Southampton, who later sold it to a preservation group. It now resides on the Bluebell Railway. Of the remaining two engines, one was cut up and the other is preserved at Bressingham in Norfolk.

Plate 30 (above):   Shawford Junction was the meeting place of the main line and the Newbury line *(see Plate 20)*, and the photograph shows the Didcot, Newbury & Southampton Railway line to the right, behind the signal box. On the main line, on 22nd May 1960, is a 'down' empty engineers' train bound for Eastleigh Yard, hauled by Class U locomotive No. 31635. During World War II, an additional connection was made between the 'up' main line and the Didcot, Newbury & Southampton line north of Winchester, to avoid congestion at Shawford Junction. At the same time, an extra line for 'down' trains from Newbury was added, from Shawford Junction to a point just north of Eastleigh. This line ran round the back of Shawford Station, and was therefore of no use for passenger trains. These two additional lines were built to cope with the extensive troop and armament movements to Southampton. Shawford Junction has now been taken out, but the 'down' wartime line now forms the 'down' relief line for Waterloo to Bournemouth trains, and a platform for this line has been added at Shawford Station.

Plate 29 (left lower):   The sub-shed at Winchester was of a size to match the Class B4 locomotive, and was constructed of corrugated iron by the Southern Railway. One of these engines had been allocated here for many years, although for a short time in 1958, an ex-SECR Class P, No. 31325, was tried. Because of the tight curves in the yard, it was found unsuitable, and a B4 locomotive was soon reinstated. It remained here until its withdrawal in 1963, being replaced by a small diesel shunter. The yard closed completely in 1969.

Plate 31 (overleaf):   Winchester (Chesil), on the evening of 22nd May 1960, saw a Ramblers' excursion headed by Class E1, locomotive No. 31067. The train was returning to London Bridge from Eastleigh via the Didcot, Newbury & Southampton line and Reading, then back on to the Southern system. The regular service was operated jointly by the Southern and Western regions, thus providing a considerable variety of motive power and stock. Trains operated on weekdays only, and ran from Southampton Terminus to Newbury. Connections to and from Didcot were very poor, despite the original name of the railway, and the line was built with the hope that it would become a trunk route from the Midlands to Southampton Docks. In the event, it became little more than a branch line, partly because of its failure, for financial and political reasons, to progress beyond Winchester as an independent company. In addition, it faced competition from the Midland & South Western Junction Railway from Cheltenham, which was also a north to south route, joining the LSWR system at Andover. Winchester Chesil Station slowly died, and passenger services north to Newbury ceased two months before this photograph was taken. However, the line south to Shawford Junction had a reprieve, and on summer Saturdays in the following year, it was used as the terminus for the diesel trains from Southampton. It was not closed completely until April 1966.

Plate 33 (right upper):   An 'up' parcels train, on the evening of 22nd May 1960, with Shawford Station visible in the background. The engine is 'West Country' class, No. 34095 *Brentor*, and the stock comprises mostly LMSR bogie brake vehicles. The extra 'down' Newbury to Southampton line can be seen on the far left *(see Plate 30)*.

Plate 32 (above):   More unusual motive power is pictured between Winchester (Chesil) and Shawford Junction, in the form of Class B4 locomotive, No. 30096. On 9th March and again on 6th April 1963, this engine worked a special passenger train to Southampton Docks. On the first occasion, the weather was very poor, with drizzle and low cloud all day, but on the April trip the day was clear if somewhat crisp, as seen in this view. When the Didcot, Newbury & Southampton Railway was opened in 1885, it terminated at Winchester, then known as Cheese Hill Station. The section from Winchester to Shawford Junction was opened six years later and was operated by the LSWR, which was thus able to dictate terms for the conveyance of traffic on to Southampton Docks.

Plate 34 (right lower):   With a train of empty oil wagons on 6th April 1963, Class 4MT, No. 76011 makes its way to Fawley on the edge of Southampton Water, where there is a large refinery. In the background is Eastleigh Station, and to the right is Eastleigh Carriage & Wagon Works. The works was built by the LSWR in 1889 to replace facilities at Nine Elms. Although the works is now closed, some of the main buildings are in use by private companies. The BR Class 4MT 76XXX locomotives were introduced in 1953, and Nos. 76005-19 were allocated to the Southern Region, mainly for use in Hampshire to replace pre-grouping engines.

EASTLEIGH RUNNING SHED AND WORKS

Plate 35: The quickest route from Eastleigh Station to the running shed and the locomotive works, which can be seen in the background, was along the permanent way. A notice forbidding this practice was prominently displayed at the end of the 'up' platform. This notice was still in position long after electrification. Approaching the station, on 25th July 1956, is "King Arthur' class, No 30770 *Sir Prianius*, with the 5p.m. Bournemouth West to Waterloo train. A portion from Weymouth was attached at Bournemouth Central.

Plate 36: Apart from scheduled trains, there were, in the Eastleigh area, many light engine workings with transfers between the shed and works or the extensive marshalling yards at the London end of the station. Coupled together on a wet day in April 1961, are Class T9, No 30117, and BR Standard Class 3MT, No 82012, seen running towards the station. The overbridge leads to a wide cul-de-sac, lined on one side by railwaymen's houses, and its purpose was to provide road access to the locomotive works and running shed.

Plate 37:   Eastleigh Running Shed was one of the most important and largest on the Southern system, and had an allocation of well over 100 engines for much of its existence. The shed was built in 1903 to replace the one at Northam, just outside Southampton, and had fifteen through roads and a large coaling ramp. It was extraordinary that a shed of such importance, which included express 4-6-0 tender engines in its allocation, had only a 55ft. turntable resulting in large engines being turned on a triangle at the opposite end of the shed. A general view of the shed, on 23rd December 1965, shows a preponderance of Standard locomotives and one USA tank engine, No. 30071. Behind No. 30071 is Class 4MT locomotive, No. 75077 and to the left is another Class 4MT, No. 80102. There is very little inside the shed which, within two years, had closed. The shed roads have since been relaid for stabling diesel and electric multiple units.

Plate 38:   Until the last years of steam, Eastleigh Shed was very busy every day of the week, and one could always be assured of seeing a variety of motive power, from old LSWR engines to Bulleid Pacifics, many of which were built at the nearby locomotive works. Outside the shed on 1st November 1955, only a month prior to withdrawal, is Class D15, No. 30465. The D15 locomotives were one of several classes of express passenger engines built by Drummond. Only ten of this class were built, but they were the largest and the last of his 4-4-0s. They were used on the Salisbury and Bournemouth line and then on the London to Portsmouth line, almost until electrification in 1937. Even in their last years, they were still used regularly on boat trains from Waterloo to Lymington Pier (*see Plate 95*).

Plate 39: The condemned road at Eastleigh Shed was nearly always full, and on this occasion, in May 1960, three Class T9 4-4-0 locomotives and two 'King Arthurs' are seen there. In the foreground are Nos. 30287 and 30117, although they were later reprieved *(see Plate 36),* and were not withdrawn until the following year. The author recalls arriving at Eastleigh from Portsmouth in 1955, behind Class T9 No. 30732. During a visit to the works he had occasion to explore the rear, where he was assured there was nothing but scrap-iron. To his disbelief, he came across the main frames and cab of a Class T9 engine, quite clearly numbered 30732. The explanation is that during the previous year, Eastleigh had taken the frames of No. 30722 and fitted to these sufficient of the original locomotive No. 30732 to produce a locomotive now numbered 30732, which was returned to traffic and survived until 1959. The underframes of the original No. 30732, no longer required, were left at the rear of the works until cutting up took place in 1957. The tall building in the background is the diesel maintenance depot, built for the 'Hampshire' units. It was these units that displaced the Class T9 engines, which were used with passenger trains on the secondary routes radiating from Eastleigh.

Plate 40: On a less morbid note, Class T9 No. 120 is seen at Eastleigh Shed on 11th November 1962. This engine was overhauled and repainted in LSWR green during the previous year. It was used on special trains for a couple of years, and during summer Saturdays of 1962 it frequently worked the scheduled Waterloo to Basingstoke trains. It is now part of the National Collection. To the left of No. 120 is 'Schools' class locomotive No. 30926 *Repton.*

Plate 41: Members of the 0415 class were only seen at Eastleigh for overhauls, and otherwise spent all their time based at Exmouth Junction Shed for operating the Lyme Regis branch. On 8th July 1961 No. 30584 was on the condemned road at Eastleigh Shed, having lost its numberplate and looking decidedly forlorn. It had been at Eastleigh since the beginning of the year, following replacement of all three of the class at Exmouth Junction by Ivatt 2-6-2 tank engines. It was finally broken up a year after its last journey to Eastleigh. No. 30582 was broken up the same year, but No. 30583 was purchased by the Bluebell Railway, where it can still be seen.

Plate 42: The LSWR opened Eastleigh Works in 1908 for both the building and repair of locomotives. The first engines to be built there were two Class S14s *(see Plate 79)*, and the first tender engines were Drummond 4-6-0s. During World War II Eastleigh produced some Stanier Class 8F locomotives for the War Department and a variety of items unrelated to railways such as fighting vehicles and armaments. In British Railways' days, the works was responsible for the repair of the region's ex-LMSR and Standard classes, locomotives of LSWR and SR origin and, after closure of Brighton Works, some of the ex-LBSCR locomotives. As the modernization plan progressed, the works also took responsibility for repairs to diesel and electric traction units. Many of the components for Standard locomotives being built elsewhere were manufactured at Eastleigh. The locomotive works later became part of British Rail Engineering Ltd. Inside the erecting shop, on 22nd May 1960, are two 700 class 0-6-0 tender engines, Nos. 30697 and 30316. Despite being of a Drummond design, this class of thirty engines was built by Dubs of Glasgow. They were rebuilt at Eastleigh from 1920, which resulted in less attractive but more efficient engines. The first withdrawal was not until 1957, and this was the result of accident damage. The remainder of the class was withdrawn between 1959 and 1962.

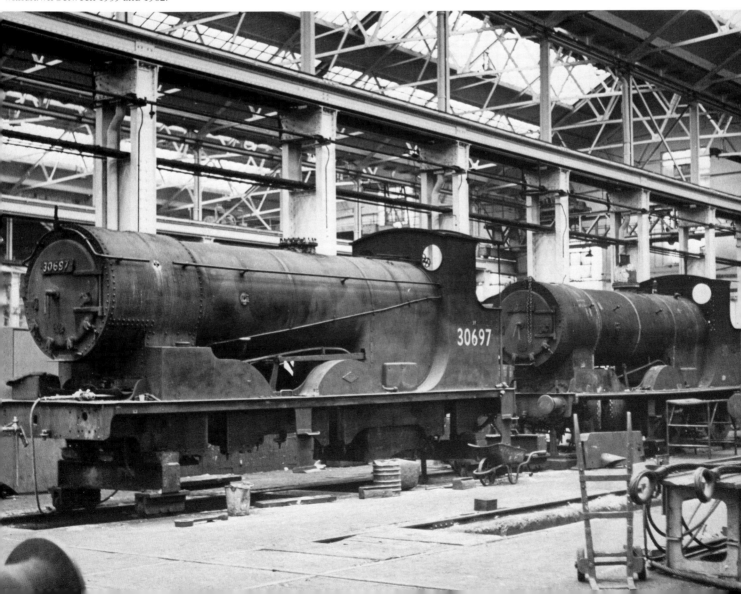

Plate 45 (right upper): The Southern Railway inherited a few engines from minor railways, in which were included three tank engines from the Plymouth Devonport & South Western Junction Railway. All were built by Hawthorn Leslie & Co., one an 0-6-0 and the remainder being 0-6-2 locomotives. After amalgamation, the 0-6-0 locomotive was used for shunting duties on various part of the Southern system whilst the other two engines, now known as Class 757, remained on home territory, being allocated to Plymouth for working freight trains to Callington. They spent most of their time, from 1952, out of use at Plymouth Shed until mid-1956, when they were both transferred to Eastleigh, ostensibly to act as works' pilots. No. 30758 *Lord St. Levan* was, however, almost immediately condemned, but No. 30757 *Earl of Mount Edgcumbe* was seen shunting in the works on 25th July 1956.

Plate 43: 'Merchant Navy' Pacific No. 35006 *Peninsular & Oriental S. N. Co.* is pictured in the works on 5th August 1959. It was built at Eastleigh in December 1941 and numbered 21C6 in accordance with Bulleid nomenclature. The front and rear bogies were assigned numbers corresponding to the number of axles, and the driving wheels were similarly lettered. In the photograph, the engine is undergoing rebuilding, which between 1956 and 1959 was carried out on the whole class. No. 35006 was withdrawn in 1964 and spent many years thereafter languishing at Barry in South Wales with several other members of the class, but in 1982 it was removed from Barry, pending restoration.

Plate 44: A most unusual visitor to Eastleigh Works on the occasion of the 1957 'Open Day' was an ex LBSCR Class H2 Atlantic. It was the more powerful of the two classes of Atlantic locomotives designed by Marsh, and bore many similarities to the GNR engines. No. 32424 was named *Beachy Head*. The H2 class engines were built at Brighton Works in 1911/2, and allocated to Brighton Shed for most of their life. They worked express passenger trains and, in particular, boat trains between Victoria and Newhaven. They were all withdrawn by 1956 except the one shown here, which, in its last years, was used on inter-regional trains. It was withdrawn in 1958.

Plate 46 (right lower): The end of an express locomotive. 'King Arthur' class No. 30750 was named *Morgan Le Fay*, at least until a few days before this photograph was taken in August 1957. This was one of the original LSWR 'King Arthur' class locomotives *(see Plate 15)*, all of which were condemned by 1958. Most of their duties were taken over by BR Standard Class 5MT engines, to whom the names were transferred *(see Plate 4)*.

EASTLEIGH TO ALTON

Plate 47: On 8th November 1957, an Alton train consisting of Class M7 No. 30480 and two LSWR coaches, is ready to leave Eastleigh. Most trains from Alton terminated at Eastleigh, although one late afternoon train ran on to Southampton Terminus. The original station on this site was known as Bishopstoke but was renamed Eastleigh & Bishopstoke in 1889 and was rebuilt just before the turn of the century. Although the building was of the same basic style as Micheldever *(see Plate 24)*, it had a rather unusual layout, in that there was only one exit and both platforms were islands. Booking facilities were not at ground level, but on the footbridge leading to the platforms. There were two centre through roads, with the inner faces of the platforms used predominantly by main line stopping trains. Portsmouth and Romsey trains used the outer platforms.

Plate 48: Trains to Alton traversed the main line until reaching Winchester Junction, two miles north of Winchester Station. They then ran for a short distance on the 'down' main line before the junction for the Alton line proper, which followed the Itchen Valley for much of its course. All the stations except Medstead & Four Marks were built to the same attractive design, and the photograph shows Alresford in 1966, seven years before its closure by British Railways. The station is virtually unchanged today, and forms part of the Mid-Hants Railway.

Plate 49: Alton was the terminal point for services from Eastleigh, although it was a through station on the line to Brookwood and Waterloo. Class M7, No. 30028 waits to leave with a 'down' train, in October 1957. Alton was also the starting point for trains to Basingstoke, and to Fareham via the Meon Valley, all three lines diverging at Butts Junction on the steep climb out of Alton. The Basingstoke line was closed in 1936, except for a short length retained to serve a local hospital. The Meon Valley line was built to main line standards, and was intended to offer a direct service from Waterloo to Stokes Bay (Gosport) for the Isle of Wight *(see Plate 56)*. The traffic never materialized, as a result of the LSWR gaining access to Portsmouth Harbour, so the line became nothing more than a branch, eventually closing in 1955. The line from Alton to Butts Junction was double, but once the electric train service from Waterloo to Alton was introduced, this section was operated as two independent single lines, one for the Meon Valley trains and the other for Eastleigh trains.

Plate 50: A special train at Alton, again with Class M7, No. 30028 and, apart from the headboard, indistinguishable from an ordinary service train. The train is leaving for Farringdon on 15th October 1960, which was all that remained of the Meon Valley line, and which was operated as a siding from Alton for local goods traffic. The special also ran on the remnants of the Basingstoke line to Treloar's Hospital.

Plate 53 (right upper): Botley, betwee[n] Eastleigh and Fareham, was the junctio[n] for a branch to Bishop's Waltham. Th[e] was only three and a half miles long, an[d] was opened in 1863, an intermediate ha[lt] being added at Durley in 1910. The lin[e] closed to passenger services in 1933, bu[t] remained open for freight until 196[2.] Occasional special trains were seen on th[e] line, and on 7th March 1959, Class M[7] No. 30111 is waiting to propel its train t[o] Bishop's Waltham as part of a tour o[f] Hampshire branch lines. Botley Statio[n] buildings were replaced by a shelter i[n] 1969, and the Bishop's Waltham bay wa[s] used for roadstone trains in conjunctio[n] with motorway construction in the area.

Plate 51: Signal boxes were usually readily attributable to a particular railway by virtue of their style. The LSWR had a number of standard designs, depending on their size and the period during which they were built. The small country box, such as the one at Medstead & Four Marks, was to be found over all parts of the system, with minor variations depending on the availability of local materials. This was particularly noticable in the West Country, where the bases were built of stone rather than brick.

Plate 52: The signal box at Alton was much more modern in appearance, as well as being somewhat larger. Alton Station was opened in 1852, but was resited in 1865 on the opening of the Winchester line. Further major changes occurred in 1903, in conjunction with the opening of the Meon Valley line, these including the provision of a new signal box and rearranged platforms. Electrification from London in 1937 resulted in the lengthening of the platforms, and the enlargement of the box.

Plate 54 (right lower): There was, at on[e] time, a plan to build a railway fro[m] Bishop's Waltham to Petersfield, but th[is] never materialized and in the en[d] Bishop's Waltham was served only by t[he] branch from Botley. In the heyday of t[he] branch, there was a motor train servic[e] which ran approximately every ho[ur] during weekdays and even provided [a] Sunday service. For a short while, trai[ns] were operated by the then recently bu[ilt] Class C14 locomotives *(see Plate 79)*, b[ut] these were later replaced by the M7 clas[s.] However, a C14 did reappear at Bishop['s] Waltham many years later, with [a] railway enthusiasts' special. On 7th March 1959, another special paid a sho[rt] visit.

Plate 55:   Fareham can also be reached by leaving the main Southampton line at St. Denys. This is a much slower route than that from Eastleigh to Fareham, by virtue of the numerous intermediate stations and the circuitous nature of the line. Shortly after leaving St. Denys, the line crosses the River Itchen and then runs along its east bank almost to Southampton Water. At Bursledon, it crosses the River Hamble which, incidentally, flows through both Botley and Bishop's Waltham. Inter-regional traffic, notably from the west and Wales, usually took the St. Denys line to Portsmouth. On 6th August 1958 Class U, No. 31794 works the 2.45p.m Portsmouth & Southsea to Bristol (Temple Meads) service through St. Denys. The station is situated in the 'vee' of the junction, and thus has separate platforms on the main and Fareham lines.

Plate 56:   Another cross-country train, this time at Fareham, on 30th April 1961. This is the 10.10a.m. Plymouth to Portsmouth & Southsea train, and consists of a mixture of LMSR and SR stock, hauled by 'Battle of Britain' class, No. 34049 *Anti-Aircraft Command*. At Fareham, the Portsmouth line turns sharply east, whereas the Gosport branch continues straight on, giving the impression that the latter is the main line. Indeed, it was envisaged as such, being a continuation of the Meon Valley line from Alton to Stokes Bay *(see Plate 49).*

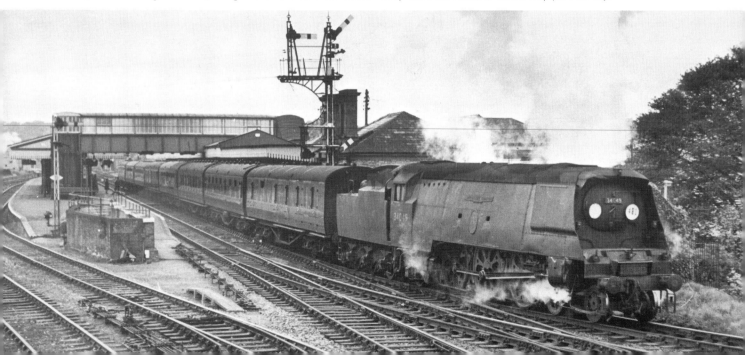

Plate 57: In contrast to the previous plate, another train on the same day was hauled by two pre-grouping tank engines, and is seen here just north of Fareham on the Meon Valley line. The engines are ex-LBSCR Class E1, No. 32694 and ex-LSWR Class 02, No. 30200. The short distance between Fareham and the point where the Meon Valley and Eastleigh lines diverged at Knowle has had a history of continual change. Until the Meon Valley line was built, the Eastleigh line entered Fareham through a tunnel. Because the immediate area was rather unstable, a line avoiding the tunnel from Knowle Junction was built, three years after the Meon Valley line was opened. The tunnel was used only by Alton trains, with the Eastleigh trains using the new line. In 1907, a halt was opened at Knowle, but could only be used by trains on the tunnel route because the junction had been taken out. It was reinstated in 1921, and from then until 1962, both routes could be used by all trains. In 1962, the Eastleigh-bound deviation became blocked by a landslip, necessitating further operating rearrangements. Two years later, the halt was closed and then in 1973, the deviation was closed to all traffic, and trains now use the tunnel route.

Plate 58: The line running east from Fareham meets, at Portcreek Junction, at the northern end of Portsea Island, the main Waterloo to Portsmouth Harbour line which has been electrified since 1937. Approaching Fratton, between this junction and Portsmouth, on 30th April 1961, is an electric train from Brighton. The front unit is 2HAL, No. 2663, built by the Southern Railway at Eastleigh in 1939 for the London to Maidstone and Gillingham services. In the siding is Class T9, No. 30117, waiting to run down to Portsmouth Harbour to work a passenger train. In 1885 a branch, a little over a mile long, was opened from Fratton to Southsea. There was a proposal to connect it to Hayling Island by a bridge across Langston Harbour, but this was abandoned. The branch was operated by steam railcars, but only lasted until 1914. The electric train depot, built in 1937, *(see Plate 59)* was located close to the course of the branch as it turned sharply south, away from the main line at Fratton.

Plate 59: Fratton Shed was responsible for providing motive power for the cross-country services originating from Portsmouth, and therefore had an allocation of several passenger engines. Fratton also provided motive power for the Hayling Island branch. Early on the morning of 3rd November 1963, two ex-LBSCR 'Terriers', Nos. 32636 and 32670 are waiting to leave Fratton for Havant, to work the Hayling Island trains.

32670

Plate 60 (left upper): Fratton Shed was closed in 1959, but was used as a stabling point for some years after this. It was also used to store several locomotives pending their preservation. On 8th September 1963 these included one of the famous Beattie well tanks, No. 30587. There were originally twelve of these engines, built by Beyer Peacock & Co. for use on London suburban services. They were known as Class 329, and all except three were withdrawn by 1898. The survivors were rebuilt successively by Adams, Urie and Maunsell and miraculously survived into British Railways' ownership. They were used exclusively on the Wenfordbridge branch in Cornwall, until withdrawal in 1963. No. 30587 now forms part of the National Collection and one of the others, No. 30585, has also survived.

Plate 62 (above): There were extensive electric train sidings and sheds at Fratton. Tucked inconspicuously down the side of the sheds, on 30th April 1961, was unit No. 93. This was one of several trains which usually only operated during the winter hours of darkness on conductor rail de-icing duties. The headcode '08' signifies Portsmouth to Waterloo non-stop, and the bar over the numbers indicates that the train is empty stock. The units were converted from ordinary electric passenger stock, and survived their contemporaries in revenue-earning service by many years. The two coaches in unit No. 93 were the motor coaches of three coach suburban set No. 1510, built in 1925. In common with all these sets, an extra coach, usually of Bulleid design, was added after World War II, this particular set becoming No. 4340. The conversions to de-icing units were carried out at Stewarts Lane in 1960, and were to replace the ex-LBSCR trailer coaches, which were propelled by ordinary electric units.

Plate 61 (left lower): One of the Lancing Works shunters, Class A1 No. DS680, is seen under repair at Fratton on 30th April 1961. This engine was built at Brighton Works in 1876 as No. 54 and was named *Waddon*. It was sold in 1904 to the SECR and renumbered 751, but was renumbered in the departmental series in 1932. In 1963 it was displaced from Lancing, together with No. DS681, by USA class tank engines which were surplus to requirements at Southampton Docks *(see Plates 77 & 78)*. Although it was reboilered several times, it was never formally rebuilt as a Class A1X. Following withdrawal, it was shipped to Canada and is now preserved in Montreal.

Plate 63: Class A1X, No. 32650 is pictured leaving Havant, with the 10.35a.m. train to Hayling Island on 8th September 1963. The LBSCR reached Havant in 1847 via the coast route to Portsmouth, followed twelve years later by the arrival of the LSWR main line from Waterloo. By comparison with these lines, the railway, which was opened in 1867 to Hayling Island, was insignificant. No engines larger than Class A1X could be used on the line, and even with these engines, double-heading was not permitted, due to restrictions on Langston Bridge. The speed limit on the line was 35 m.p.h., reduced to 20 m.p.h. on the bridge.

Plate 64: A Class A1X, engine No. 32662 is seen at work on the Hayling Island line on 11th November 1963, the last day of services. The centre coach is the unique fibreglass-bodied vehicle, built at Eastleigh in the previous year. The line ran across very exposed land on the edge of Langston Harbour and, on a number of occasions, suffered storm damage. There was, for a short time in the 1880s, a ferry service connecting Langston with Brading Harbour on the Isle of Wight with rail connections at both ends, but this ran into financial difficulties and was abandoned. It was, however, no great loss to the branch, as passenger traffic grew steadily as Hayling Island developed as a holiday resort.

Plate 65: Class AIX No. 32650 is pictured near Langston Bridge on 10th October 1963. The first road link with the mainland was over a narrow toll bridge, which probably helped to arrest the post-war decline in passengers. A new road bridge was opened in 1958, but the railway continued to offer an excellent service, with main line connections at Havant. On summer Saturdays, many of the trains ran non-stop between Havant and Hayling Island.

Plate 66: On 21st August 1960 the 3.05p.m. Havant to Hayling Island train is hauled by Class AIX No. 32670. This engine had only recently been transferred to Fratton Shed, and still displays the code 74E of its former home of St. Leonards where it had been used to work the freight only line of the former Kent & East Sussex Railway, between Robertsbridge and Tenterden.

Plate 67 (left upper): Two years previously almost to the day found most of the rolling stock still of pre-grouping vintage, although the first signs of a new order can be seen on the rear of the train. The coach in the foreground is ex-LSWR composite, No. 4753, and the engine standing by the primitive coaling stage at Hayling Island is No. 32640. This was one of several Class A1X locomotives sold to the Isle of Wight Central Railway, and it remained on the Isle of Wight until 1947. It was withdrawn in 1963 and sold to Butlins, but ultimately returned to the Isle of Wight and may now be seen at Haven Street.

Plate 69 (above): With no sign of pre-grouping coaches in August 1960, the modern image was rather incongruously relieved by an 88 year old engine, No. 32670. The main drawback to using the train was that Hayling Island Station was some distance from the most popular holiday area of the Island, thereby necessitating a long walk or a journey by taxi or bus. After closure, there was a privately-sponsored scheme to operate the line as a tramway and for some years, a single decker tram from Blackpool was stored in the yard at Havant. The plan was later abandoned, and most of the branch has since been dismantled.

Plate 68 (left lower): Although passengers formed the bulk of business on the Hayling Island branch, there was some freight activity even at the height of the holiday season. In August 1958, No. 32640 attends to a few wagons at Hayling Island. Many years previously, freight traffic was transferred from rail to ship at Langston Quay, but as the harbour silted up this was abandoned. Freight continued to be handled at Hayling Island until the line was closed in 1963.

EASTLEIGH TO ANDOVER AND SALISBURY

Plate 70: Leaving Eastleigh in a westerly direction is the line for Romsey, and immediately prior to entering Romsey Station is the junction with the line from Southampton. Three miles beyond Romsey the railway forked, one line continuing westwards to Salisbury and the other northwards to Andover, both joining the West of England main line. All of these lines were included in the Southern Region dieselization programme, and apart from inter-regional and other long-distance trains, steam was only occasionally seen in this area after 1957. Even these trains eventually succumbed to diesel traction, and the sight of a Class T9 locomotive with a train of LSWR coaches was just a memory. However, steam returned briefly on 17th September 1966 in the form of two BR Standard Class 4MT locomotives, Nos. 80152 and 80016, pictured near Chandler's Ford, between Eastleigh and Romsey.

Plate 71: Railtours were usually conspicuous by the special headboards which adorned the locomotive, sometimes to excess. Class 700 No. 30309 is seen at Fullerton Junction on a special from Salisbury to Eastleigh via Andover on 2nd September 1962. Fullerton lies between Romsey and Andover, and was a junction for another line, which ran to Hurstbourne on the West of England main line. The line was built to serve as a connection for trains from the Didcot, Newbury & Southampton Railway from Whitchurch *(see Plate 20)*, which could then reach Southampton over LSWR metals. Because the Whitchurch connection was never built, the line assumed no significant purpose and was closed to passengers in 1931. Part was, however, retained for freight traffic until 1956.

Plate 72: Another steam working, on this occasion to mark the end of services on the Andover to Romsey line, which had been diesel multiple unit-operated for seven years. Class 3MT No. 82029 is seen passing through Mottisfont, on the evening of 6th September 1964. Mottisfont Station was situated only half a mile from Kimbridge Junction, where the Andover and Salisbury lines parted company. Its counterpart on the Salisbury line was named Dunbridge, and it seems odd that a single station to serve both of the lines could not have been built at Kimbridge, where there was road access and even a level crossing, and a terrace of railway houses. Admittedly Dunbridge was opened in 1847, some eighteen years before Mottisfont, but there were many precedents for the resiting of stations as a result of changed circumstances.

Plate 73: Apart from Dunbridge, there was only one other station on the Romsey to Salisbury line. This was Dean, located in the centre of the village of West Dean, and was on the boundary with Wiltshire. The line was double track throughout, and joined the Bournemouth to Salisbury line at Alderbury Junction, four miles beyond Dean. This photograph of Dean Station, taken in April 1964, shows it to be in virtually original condition.

Plate 74: In complete contrast to Dean was Braemore, located on the Bournemouth to Salisbury line. It was a most unattractive station, despite its proximity to the fine country house of the same name. The line, which was opened in 1866, was single track from Alderbury Junction to West Moors, where it joined the line from Brockenhurst *(see Plate 109)*. Rather unusually for a country station, the Southern Railway provided electric lighting. It was closed in May 1964, two weeks after this photograph was taken.

SALISBURY TO BOURNEMOUTH

Plate 75: Although the closure of branch lines was, in many cases, seen as inevitable due to the vast increase in car ownership, and the fact that stations were often remote from the villages they served, closure of main stations was something altogether more surprising. In Hampshire, two stations, both in large towns with substantial passenger traffic, closed in the 1960s, one being Bournemouth West *(see Plate 125)* and the other Southampton Terminus. The latter was opened in 1839 as Southampton, the terminus of the main line from Waterloo. Its name changed a few years later to Southampton Docks, then to Southampton Town & Docks, Southampton Town for Docks and finally, at amalgamation, to Southampton Terminus. Several factors contributed to its decline, which took place over many years. It began with the extension of the line to Bournemouth and the new station on the through line at Southampton West. This was followed by the expansion of the town of Southampton towards the west, and with the ever diminishing passenger traffic, it finally served no useful purpose. Class 4MT, No. 76069 is pictured in the last days of this once busy station, on 21st December 1965, waiting to leave with the 1.16p.m. train to Weymouth. The station closed to passenger services on 5th September 1966 and to all traffic in March 1968. The main building still stands, as it is the subject of a preservation order.

SOUTHAMPTON DOCKS

Plate 76: Entry into Southampton Docks for boat trains was by a line which ran alongside Southampton Terminus and over the public highway, at the appropriately named Canute Road. On 6th April 1963, ex-LSWR Class B4, No. 30096 hauls a passenger train into the docks, under the direction of a flag man. Behind the engine are the offices of the Union Castle Line, after which 'Merchant Navy' class, No. 35002 was named. Southampton Docks was purchased from the company of the same name by the LSWR in 1892. Included in the purchase were several small shunting engines, one of which, named *Ironside*, was later used as the Guildford Shed pilot. History repeated itself, because at both Southampton and Guildford, *Ironside* was displaced by a Class B4 locomotive. The same fate was to befall these engines which themselves were replaced by USA tanks at both locations, many years later.

Plate 77: In 1946, the Southern Railway obtained, through the War Department, fifteen American-built 0-6-0 tank engines. Only fourteen entered SR stock, as Nos. 61-74, and the other locomotive was used for spares. This effectively ended the monopoly of the Class B4 tank engines, as the majority were allocated to Southampton Docks Shed, to which British Railways gave the code 71I. The USA class tanks could be seen working in all parts of the docks right up to the introduction of diesel shunters in 1962. No. 30065 is shunting a BR brake third coach, to form part of an 'up' boat train, the destination board on the coach declaring 'Waterloo to Southampton Docks'. In the background can be seen the funnels of an ocean liner.

Plate 78: Another USA tank, No. 30062, is seen outside the docks running shed on 1st November 1955. The first shed on the site was owned by the Southampton Docks Co., and was successively enlarged and rebuilt by its subsequent owners, including British Railways who fitted a new roof in 1955. There was also a shed at Southampton Terminus, but this was closed many years before the end of steam. The docks shed was retained for the diesel shunters, and was not closed until 1966.

Plate 79: It may come as a surprise to learn that the Southern Railway possessed other locomotives as small as their Class B4. The C14 class, also of Drummond origin, was intended for push-pull operation. Unfortunately, their performance was little better than the railcars they were designed to replace, and they were relegated to light shunting duties even as far back as 1912. They were originally built as 2-2-0s and although rebuilt as 0-4-0s, they were still only capable of performing the least taxing of duties. Several were sold to the Government during World War I, but three passed into British Railways hands in 1948. A Class C14 tank was often to be seen shunting on Southampton Quay, and taking a rest between duties, on 7th August 1957, is No. 30588. The engine was first numbered 741, then 0741 on the duplicate list, 3741 in 1935 and finally 30588. It was withdrawn at the end of 1957. Drummond also built the S14 class, very similar in appearance to the Class C14 tanks and for the same purpose, but with four coupled wheels from the outset. There were only two of these engines, and they were both sold in 1917.

Plate 80: Other small locomotives used in the docks included the Adams Class O2 passenger engines. No. 30229 is pictured shunting on the quay on 3rd August 1957. There were sixty of these engines, which were used on branch lines throughout the LSWR, including the Bishop's Waltham line *(see Plate 54)*. Commencing in 1923, about a third of the class were modified for use on the Isle of Wight, where one can still be seen. Both the mainland and island engines continued to operate passenger trains well into British Railways' days, until closure or the arrival of modern motive power rendered them redundant.

Plate 81: Southampton New Docks, which was built on reclaimed land and opened in 1934, was owned by the Southern Railway from the outset. Although there was no formal running shed, there was a locomotive servicing point. In the New Docks, on 1st November 1955, are ex-LBSCR 0-6-0 goods engine Class E1, No. 32606, and USA tank, No. 30066. Not only did the Southern Railway operate ancient locomotives, but they also had two steam lorries for use in the docks. One of these was still working on the day this photograph was taken.

Plate 82: Southampton New Docks was also used as a stabling point for passenger trains which started from Southampton Central. On 1st November 1955 Class T9 No. 30729 and Bulleid set No. 784 are seen waiting to form the 4.05p.m. Southampton Central to Fareham train. In the last few years rail traffic from the docks has decreased dramatically. The succession of boat trains following the arrival of ocean liners is virtually a thing of the past, although boat trains are still run in connection with cruises from Southampton. Freight traffic is also negligible by comparison with pre-war activity, although there is a Freightliner depot at Millbrook.

Plate 83: The 'up' starters at Southampton Central Station, both made of old bullhead rail by the Southern Railway, are seen in this view with water-columns of the same vintage in the background. An 'up' freight train, hauled by Class U No. 31791 waits on the far line, whilst 'Hampshire' diesel unit No. 1118 leaves with a Salisbury to Portsmouth & Southsea train. Behind the photographer the line becomes double track through a short tunnel, before meeting the line from Southampton Terminus and reverting to four tracks. The first station on the Southampton to Dorchester line, opened in 1847, was Blechynden, which was later renamed Southampton West End. The station was resited in 1892, and then called Southampton West. It was rebuilt in 1931 and four years later renamed Southampton Central, to reflect the expansion of the city.

SOUTHAMPTON TO TOTTON

Plate 84: Even in 1958 when this photograph was taken, it was uncommon to see Class T9 4-4-0 locomotives in the Southampton area, as most had been laid aside at Eastleigh *(see Plate 39)*. However, on 6th August, No. 30706 of Bournemouth heads the 6.07p.m. Southampton Terminus to Bournemouth Central train, seen passing under the impressive signal gantry at the western end of Southampton Central Station. Although the gantry has now gone, it has been acquired by the National Railway Museum.

Plate 85: The 3.50p.m. Southampton Terminus to Bournemouth Central train, is leaving Southampton on 5th August 1959, with Standard Class 4MT, No. 76067 in charge of Bulleid set No. 860. In the background is Southampton Central Station, with its characteristic clock tower. The line westward from Southampton was originally single track, but doubling was started ten years after opening. The short section from Southampton to Millbrook was later quadrupled, the outside tracks being for through trains and the centre tracks for local trains.

Plate 86 (left upper):   The background between Southampton and Redbridge was dominated by pylons, cranes and other industrial ironmongery. Class U No. 31802 is seen near Redbridge on the 1.52p.m. Cheltenham Spa to Southampton Terminus train on 5th August 1959.

TOTTON TO FAWLEY

Plate 88 (above):   The next station after Redbridge is Totton, originally named Eling Junction. This was not, however, to signify the junction for the Fawley branch, which was not opened until 74 years later by the Southern Railway, or the junction for the Romsey line, which was actually at Redbridge. The junction referred to was a short freight only line to a quay on Southampton Water. The Fawley branch is, apart from passing loops, single throughout, and runs through flat countryside close to Southampton Water. The first station was at Marchwood, a thinly populated area between Southampton Water and the New Forest. The next station served Hythe, which is somewhat larger. Unfortunately for the railway, there was a ferry from here to Southampton, which was far quicker and very much more frequent than the train. The ferry still operates, but the railway was closed to passengers in 1966. Class M7 No. 30378 is seen at Totton with the 3.51p.m. Eastleigh to Fawley train composed of ex-LSWR coaches on 6th August 1958.

Plate 87 (left lower):   One of the three Class C14 locomotives which survived into British Railways' days was taken into service stock in 1927 and renumbered from 744 to 77s. It was used exclusively for shunting at Redbridge Sleeper Depot and survived until 1959, five years after this photograph was taken. Redbridge is situated on the River Test, two and a half miles west of Southampton Central Station, a sub-shed being provided here, compatible with the size of the engine.

BROCKENHURST TO LYMINGTON

Plate 89 (left upper): Freight trains were more frequent on the Fawley line than passenger trains, as a result of the oil refinery at the terminus, and today the line is still open for oil trains *(see Plate 34).* Occasional special passenger trains also paid visits, such as this seven coach railway enthusiasts' train on 20th March 1966, double-headed by USA tanks Nos. 30073 and 30064. Following displacement from Southampton Docks, some of the USA tanks were put into store, and six were taken into departmental stock. One of these replaced a Class 02 locomotive at Redbridge, which itself had replaced the C14 engine a few years earlier *(see Plate 87).* Two engines were repainted, in 1964, from the conventional black to malachite green, and it is these two engines which are shown in the photograph. No. 30064 and three other members of the class are still in service on privately-owned railways.

Plate 91 (above): During busy periods, the 'up' loop at Brockenhurst was also used. Trains were usually propelled to Lymington, and engines ran back chimney first on the return journey. An ex-SR set of LSWR design, converted to push-pull operation and numbered 384, was regularly used on the line. An all third coach No. 1098, which was push-pull fitted was used in addition at busy periods. The Lymington branch was opened in 1858, eleven years after Brockenhurst. The first Brockenhurst Station was demolished in 1888, and a new station was constructed as part of the improvements associated with the new direct main line to Bournemouth. The station was rebuilt in 1936.

Plate 90 (left lower): The main line enters the New Forest at the once picturesque station of Lyndhurst Road, positioned on the edge of the main Southampton to Bournemouth road. It is now nothing more than a platform with waiting shelter, a fate also suffered by Beaulieu Road. However, the next station, at Brockenhurst, has changed little since Southern Railway days and is still the interchange point for the Lymington branch. Lymington trains were operated by Class M7 0-4-4 tank engines and LSWR or SR stock, except for the period immediately prior to arrival of the diesel and electric multiple units, when modern stock was used. A bay was provided on the 'down' side of Brockenhurst Station for the branch train, occupied on 30th August 1961 by Class M7, No. 30028. This is, in fact, a loop, made by extending the bay in 1936 to make the 'down' platform an island.

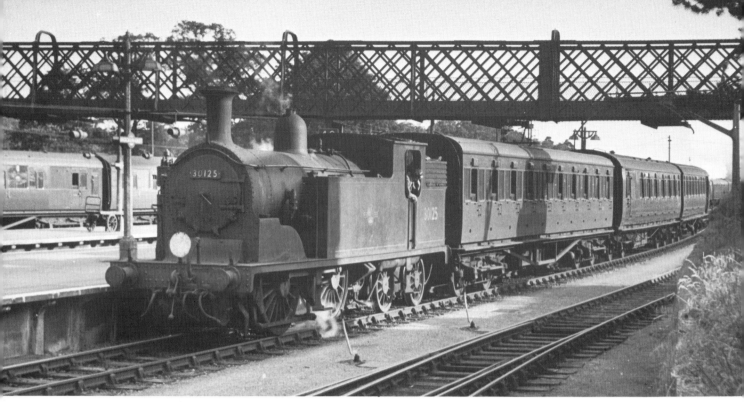

Plate 92: An evening train from Lymington, on 7th June 1960, rests in the loop after being worked by Class M7, No. 30125. Even after electrification, the branch has undergone changes. It is now operated completely independently from the main line, with the removal of the junction which was one mile west of Brockenhurst.

Plate 93: There once was a daily freight working on the Lymington branch, and on 10th September 1959, it is seen approaching the junction with the main line. The engine is SR Class Q, No. 30541, but none of the covered wagons are of Southern Railway constituent company origin. The long wheelbase van is a GWR passenger fruit van, the other covered vans are ex-LMSR and the brake van is to an LNER design. This part of the New Forest is now only heathland and although quite attractive in summer, is rather bleak in the winter months. It was near here that a halt was opened in 1860, to serve the hamlet of Shirley Holmes. It never appeared in the public timetable, and was only open during daylight hours. It closed when the direct main line to Bournemouth was opened, and the residents of Shirley Holmes were then expected to use the new station at Sway.

Plate 94: Lymington Town Station is very well positioned, close to the town centre. It was an attractive building with an all-over roof, but this was removed in 1965. There was also a sub-shed of Eastleigh here, which housed the branch engine overnight. The Town Station was originally the terminus of the line, but 26 years after opening the line was extended to the Pier, which is about half a mile round the edge of the harbour. Connections were provided with the Isle of Wight ferries, which are maintained to the present day. Class M7 No. 30125 basks in the evening sun.

Plate 95: The line between the Town and Pier stations crosses the Lymington River, then runs along the east bank, as shown in this photograph of the branch train on 4th August 1966. The train consists of Class 4MT No. 80032 and a three coach Bulleid set. Since the 1950s there have been through trains from Waterloo on summer Saturdays, these usually being worked throughout by the same engine *(see Plate 38)*. There were no turning facilities at the Pier, and engines therefore had to travel light to Brockenhurst prior to the return working, where there was a turntable and servicing facilities.

Plate 97 (right upper):   Brockenhurst was one of the most interesting stations in Hampshire and offered a variety of motive power, from the humble branch engine to Bulleid Pacifics. On 7th August 1960, the 6.07p.m. Southampton Terminus to Bournemouth Central train is seen leaving Brockenhurst, with a mere three coaches of set No 248 and an SR four-wheeled utility van, hauled by Standard Class 4MT, No. 76054. It left Southampton Central three minutes behind the 'Royal Wessex', but arrived at Bournemouth 31 minutes later than the express, after stopping at all intermediate stations.

Plate 96 (above):   Lymington was the last steam-operated branch in the South of England, and Class 4MT, No. 80032 is seen at Lymington Pier Station, waiting to leave with the Brockenhurst train in August 1966. The lower quadrant signal post has a rather truncated appearance, emphasized by the short length of the arms.

Plate 98 (right lower):   The 'Royal Wessex', pictured on the same evening, making a brisk start from Brockenhurst with 'Merchant Navy' class, No. 35023 *Holland-Afrika Line*. This was one of the last batch of ten 'Merchant Navy' class locomotives to be built, and although authorized under the auspices of the Southern Railway, did not enter service until after nationalization. It was only nine years later that this engine was rebuilt, and only another ten years before it was withdrawn in 1967, a premature end to a powerful and magnificent machine. The 'Royal Wessex' ran from 1951 to 1967.

Plate 99: The 'Lord Nelson' class locomotives were used on many of the Bournemouth expresses before the advent of Bulleid Pacifics, and well into British Railways' days they were often used on such duties. On 7th June 1960, No. 30861 *Lord Anson* had the less onerous task of working the 5.42p.m. Bournemouth Central to Eastleigh service, which stopped at virtually all intermediate stations. It is approaching Brockenhurst with Bulleid three coach corridor set No. 966, one of the original sets built in 1945. All these sets were disbanded at the end of 1963, and some of the coaches were condemned. A brake third from an identical set is still in existence on the Mid-Hants Railway.

Plate 100: The Southern Region ran relatively light trains by comparison with the other regions and, apart from west of Exeter, double-heading was not very common on either passenger or freight trains. An unusual freight working leaves Brockenhurst in June 1960, with Standard Class 4MT, No. 76058 and Class Q, No. 30539. Brockenhurst yard, which was on the 'down' side of the main line, can be seen on the left, and the locomotive servicing area is marked by the water-tower *(see Plate 95)*.

Plate 101: 'West Country' class, No. 34043 *Combe Martin* is pictured climbing toward Lymington Junction, on a September evening in 1959, with the 5.05p.m. Southampton Terminus to Wimborne train, which ran on the main line via Bournemouth Central. The majority of Brockenhurst to Wimborne trains took the Ringwood route, although Wimborne could also be reached by changing at Bournemouth West. The junction signals can be seen in the background, and the mile post signifies that the engine is 93¾ miles from Waterloo. The stock consists of Maunsell coaches, which were formed into set No. 340 in 1958 specifically to work this service. This set was disbanded two years after the photograph was taken.

Plate 102: The last Bulleid coaches were built after nationalization, and one such three coach set, No. 864, forms the 5.43p.m. Southampton Central to Bournemouth West via Ringwood train on 10th September 1959, headed by Standard Class 4MT, No. 76014. Set No. 864 was later reduced to one brake third and a composite coach, and was used on the Swanage portion of the 'Royal Wessex' until 1963. The Ringwood line left the direct line to Bournemouth at the same point as the Lymington branch.

BROCKENHURST TO BOURNEMOUTH (VIA RINGWOOD)

Plate 104 (right upper):   Another Class M7, No. 30106, is seen just beyond Lymington Junction on 10th September 1959, with the direct mai line to Bournemouth visible on the right. The train, consisting of two coach ex-LSWR set No. 35 and a Bulleid third, is the 4.15p.m Brockenhurst to Bournemouth West via Ringwood service. This was the route of the original Southampton & Dorchester Railway, which swun inland at this point because Ringwood and Wimborne were far more important than the coastal towns. Thus Bournemouth and Poole wer effectively bypassed, although a line was also built from Ringwood to Christchurch, which was later extended to Bournemouth East an eventually Bournemouth West. Waterloo to Weymouth trains, with a portion for Bournemouth, were separated at Ringwood. Once the dire main line was opened as far as Bournemouth, in 1888, Bournemouth portions were detached at Brockenhurst.

Plate 103 (above):   The Ringwood line trains were formed of two coaches for most of the day, which was more than sufficient to meet the deman for seats. Class M7, No. 30104 re-enters Brockenhurst on the main line, after its arrival in one of the bay platforms with a train fro Bournemouth West, on 7th June 1960. Immediately behind the last coach is the level crossing over the main Lyndhurst to Lymington road. Th frequent train service and shunting movements, such as the one shown in the photograph, resulted in long queues of traffic, particularly in th summer. The problem is a little better nowadays, as lifting barriers have now been installed. The corrugated iron-roofed structure on the right a pedestrian covered way from the car-park. Booking facilities were, however, only provided on the 'up' side of the line, where there is anoth entrance to the station.

Plate 105 (right lower):   The original main line passed through some pleasant countryside, particularly prior to Ringwood, and a train is seen the cutting a short distance east of Holmsley, the first station out of Brockenhurst. The engine, Class M7, No. 30058, is propelling set No. 66 but hauling an SR utility van which is not fitted for push-pull operation. The train is the 2.08p.m. Brockenhurst to Bournemouth West servic pictured on 7th June 1960.

Plate 106: Another view of set No. 662, taken on 30th August the following year. It is seen leaving Holmsley, and forms the 10.42a.m. Poole to Brockenhurst train, with Class M7, No. 30328 on the rear. The set was formed in 1942 from a BTL and CL coach removed from a three coach SECR set. The BTL was adapted for push-pull working, and the lavatories were removed to make room for other compartments. The remaining BT from the three set was later used in set No. 31 to replace a life expired LSWR coach. Set No. 31 was also used in the Bournemouth area.

Plate 107: Approaching Holmsley, early in the morning of 7th June 1960, is Class Q, No. 30539 with a freight train from Brockenhurst. Although the small yard at Holmsley was still open, the pick-up freight train only called occasionally. Holmsley was originally opened as Christchurch Road, but was renamed at the end of 1862 to coincide with the opening of the station at Christchurch, which was then the terminus of the branch from Ringwood.

Plate 108: An 'up' freight train, pictured in August 1961, again passing through Holmsley, on this occasion hauled by Standard Class 4MT, No. 76058 of Eastleigh Shed. In order to avoid congestion in the Bournemouth area, several freight trains used the Ringwood line each day. The old main line was also used by the occasional passenger train from London, almost up to its closure. This included the Channel Islands boat trains and, on summer Saturdays, through trains to Weymouth which did not have a portion for Bournemouth.

Plate 109: The 12.26p.m. Bournemouth West to Brockenhurst train leaves West Moors. Set No. 613 is a push-pull unit, but the train is being worked conventionally by a Standard 4-6-0 tender engine, No. 76015. In the background is the junction for the Salisbury line, which curves away to the left.

Plate 110 (left upper): A modern image train, with Standard Class 4MT No. 76019 and a three coach BR set, pictured at Wimborne. This originally formed the 9.32a.m. service from Brockenhurst, which terminated at Wimborne. It is seen setting back from the station into the yard to allow a train from Salisbury to Bournemouth to pass.

Plate 112 (above): On the morning of 30th August 1961 Class N 2-6-0 No. 31814 shunts in Wimborne yard while Class 4MT No. 76015 heads the 2.08p.m. from Brockenhurst to Bournemouth West, formed of a two coach push-pull set. Several wagons have been left in the station, blocking the 'down' line. Note that one of the posts of the bracket signal has no arms, but at one time this controlled a bay hidden behind No. 76015, which had closed to passenger traffic some years ago.

Plate 111 (left lower): The 2.30p.m. motor-train from Bournemouth West to Brockenhurst is propelled by Class M7 No. 30050, and is seen from the cattle pens at Wimborne on 30th August 1961. Wimborne Station was on an embankment near the centre of the town, and a market was adjacent to the station. The line from Bournemouth as far as Wimborne was kept open for freight until 1977, thirteen years after withdrawal of passenger trains, but has now been lifted and most of the station area at Wimborne has been cleared. However, the station house still stands, and the market still flourishes on Tuesdays and Fridays.

Plate 113:   Standard Class 4MT, No. 76019 has emerged from the yard at Wimborne *(see Plate 110)*, and now forms the 11.12a.m. train to Bournemouth West. It was shown in the public timetable as originating from Wimborne, as passengers who boarded it at Brockenhurst would have an hour's wait at Wimborne, unless they changed to the train from Salisbury. In the background is the signal box which had to be raised above ground level, because the station and yard were built on a curve.

Plate 114: A Standard 2-6-0 tender engine, No. 76058, with a Bulleid three coach set, enters Broadstone with the 4.07p.m. Brockenhurst to Bournemouth West train, on 30th August 1961. The original line on to Dorchester included a short branch to the western side of Poole Harbour at Hamworthy. It became apparent that receipts would be enhanced if there was a line to Poole itself, on the other side of the harbour. A branch was therefore opened from Broadstone, known at the time as Poole New Junction, to Poole in 1872. Bournemouth was reached by bus from Poole until 1874, when the line was extended to Bournemouth West. Shortly afterwards, the Hamworthy line was closed to passengers, but 'Hamworthy Goods', as it became known, remained open.

Plate 116 (right upper): Connection between the Somerset & Dorset Railway and the Ringwood lines was originally at Wimborne, but the junction was resited at Broadstone in 1885, thereby giving S&D trains direct access to Bournemouth. This accounts for the style of signal box shown in the photograph, which does not reflect LSWR design, although Broadstone is an LSWR station. Coming off the S&D line in August 1961 is Class 4MT, No. 75072 of Bath (Green Park), with the 4.44p.m. Templecombe to Bournemouth West train.

Plate 115: An unusual feature of Broadstone were the starters on the 'up' platforms of both the Bournemouth and Weymouth lines. As evening approaches, on 30th August 1961, Class S15, No. 30837 pulls out of Broadstone with the 5.05p.m. Southampton Terminus to Wimborne train *(see Plate 102).*

Plate 117 (right lower): Climbing toward Broadstone from Poole, on 18th April 1964, is Class 4MT, No. 75073, with the 11.40a.m. train from Bournemouth West to Bath (Green Park). The train is an odd combination of an LNER bogie parcels van, a BR brake third and two Bulleid coaches. On the right is the main line to Hamworthy Junction, which runs on to Dorchester. In the sidings beyond is a row of condemned Maunsell coaches, these sidings also being used for stabling passenger stock which, during the height of the summer season, could not be accommodated at Bournemouth West.

Plate 118: Bournemouth Central Station, with its impressive all-over roof, had little changed at the time of writing from when this photograph was taken on 10th September 1959. The engine is 'West Country' class No. 34029 *Lundy*, pictured with the 11.16a.m. inter-regional train to Newcastle, which left the Southern Region via Basingstoke and Reading. In winter the train ran only as far as York, to where there is still a through service, although it is now diesel-hauled. It was not until 1893 that the direct line extended beyond Bournemouth to connect, without the need to reverse at Bournemouth West, with the Southampton & Dorchester Railway line at Hamworthy Junction. Once this connection was made, there was no longer any point in using the main line through Ringwood for through trains from Waterloo to Dorchester, so Bournemouth portions were, of course, no longer detached at Brockenhurst. Traffic on the old main line, and on the Ringwood to Christchurch branch, was thereafter mostly of local origin. The old main line retained its passenger service until 1964, but the branch from Ringwood closed in 1935.

Plate 119: A massive signal gantry dominated the 'up' exit from Bournemouth, and dwarfed by this structure, on 4th August 1966, is rebuilt 'Battle of Britain' class No. 34077 *603 Squadron*, seen with a Waterloo bound express. The 'down' platform at Bournemouth could accommodate two full-length trains end-on, and was, as a result, one of the longest platforms in Britain. There was a crossover at the midway point, to facilitate movements to and from the through roads. These have now been removed, but were used for non-stop trains and for short-term berthing of stock from trains originating or terminating here.

Plate 120: Bournemouth Shed, nearing the end of its life, pictured in the summer of 1966 with a rather dirty looking 'West Country' class, No. 34018 *Axminster*, and a Standard Class 4MT. It was one of the last sheds in the country with a steam allocation, and was situated at the west end of the station on the 'up' side. All trace has now gone, and the site is occupied by a car-park and offices. At this end of the station, there is now also a large concrete overbridge, carrying a new main road across the railway.

BOURNEMOUTH RUNNING SHED

Plate 121: In busier days, ten years previously, 'Lord Nelson' class, No. 30859 *Lord Hood* undergoes attention to its wheels in the shed. Visible on the left is another 'Lord Nelson'. Bournemouth had an allocation of about sixty locomotives, the vast majority of which were passenger engines. These included over a dozen Class M7 tank engines for the local branch lines, numerous Drummond 4-4-0 locomotives for secondary trains, and 'King Arthurs' and 'Lord Nelsons' for the express trains.

Plate 122 (left upper):   The 10.30a.m. train from Waterloo approaches the terminus at Bournemouth West on 10th September 1959. The engine, Class 4MT No. 75069, was attached at Bournemouth Central and is working tender first in readiness for the return journey. The train had been divided at Bournemouth Central and the front portion, with the engine from Waterloo, continued on to Weymouth. Set No. 296, consisting of six Bulleid coaches, was one of eleven identical sets built in 1947/8 especially for the Waterloo to Bournemouth trains, and included kitchen/dining cars. The sets spent all their working lives on the Bournemouth line, and were withdrawn or disbanded in 1961/5. In the background are the signals for the divergence of the lines to Poole and thence Dorchester or Broadstone, and Bournemouth Central and on to Waterloo. Between Bournemouth Central and West stations, trains passed from Hampshire into Dorset and then back to Hampshire. It is less complicated nowadays, firstly because Bournemouth West Station has long since closed, and secondly because the county boundary has been moved eastward to include Bournemouth in Dorset.

Plate 124 (above):   Climbing out of Bournemouth West past the carriage sidings, on 10th September 1959, is the 1.00p.m. train to Waterloo, hauled by 'West Country' class No. 34006 *Bude*. The climb out of this station began at 1 in 90, and was quite taxing with the heavier trains. When necessary, the engine from the incoming stock would give the departing train a helping hand to get it under way.

Plate 123 (left lower):   Class 5MT No 73019 passes Bournemouth West carriage sidings with the 12.43p.m. from Poole on 10th September 1959. The headcode is for the SDJR route, on which lamps rather than discs were used, even in daytime.

Plate 125 (below):   Bournemouth West Station, on the evening of 19th August 1961. Although by this time the days of the terminus were numbered, it was still busy in the early evening. The 'West Country' class, No. 34020 *Seaton* will take the 7.28p.m. train to Waterloo, and the Class M7, No. 30031, the 7.08p.m. train to Brockenhurst via Ringwood. The engine in the centre is Standard Class 4MT, No. 76010, which is just pulling away with the 6.48p.m. train to Templecombe, and has momentarily blotted out its starter on the signal gantry. Stock for later departures is just visible on both the far left and right of the photograph. Bournemouth West Station closed to all traffic in October 1965, following the closures of the Somerset & Dorset, Ringwood and Salisbury lines.

Plate 126 (right upper):   Fourteen miles west of Bournemouth, near Wareham, the Weymouth line enters a short cutting. On 11th April 1964, the 8.35a.m. Waterloo to Weymouth express is seen with rebuilt 'West Country' class, No. 34031 *Torrington*, in charge of three coach Bulleid set No. 816. These coaches were built by the Birmingham Railway Carriage & Wagon Co., and not by Eastleigh where most of the Bulleid stock was built, and had detailed differences from the Southern-built coaches.

Plate 127 (right lower):   Just over a mile beyond Wareham was Worgret Junction, where the Swanage line turned sharply south-east, in such a way that in a very short distance the main line to Weymouth and the Swanage line were running in almost opposite directions. On 17th April 1960, the 3.20p.m. Wareham to Swanage train passes Worgret Junction signal box, which is of typical LSWR style. The train is propelled by Class M7, No. 30111, immediately in front of which is an SR all-third coach No. 1093. The tablet catching equipment is visible to the right of the train.

Plate 128: The Swanage line passed through the open country of the Isle of Purbeck, where several tramways crossed the branch, the first being at Furzebrook. These were for carrying clay, most of which used to be transported by boat. There were, however, two interchange points with the Southern system. There was an intermediate station at Corfe Castle, which was in most picturesque surroundings on the edge of the village and was overlooked by the castle itself. The line rose steadily from Worgret to Corfe Castle at a gradient of 1 in 80, levelling out across Corfe Common, where the 2.45p.m. train from Swanage is seen on 11th April 1964, with Class 3MT, No. 82029 heading set No. 604.

Plate 129: On this occasion, trains were worked alternately by the Standard tank engine and Class M7, No. 30053. The pre-grouping engine is seen near Swanage, with the 4.57p.m. train from Wareham.

Plate 130:   The line climbs out of Swanage at a gradient of 1 in 76, and the motor-train makes hard work of this climb on 17th April 1960. The train is the 5.57p.m. to Wareham, comprising Class M7, No. 30111, loose coach No. 1093 and two coach set No. 385.

Plate 131:   Swanage was provided with a small engine shed and a turntable sufficient to accommodate a Southern Mogul. The branch engine, usually a Class M7, was stabled here overnight and on 11th April 1964 was No. 30053, seen returning to the station after taking coal and water.

Plate 132 (below):   In the summer, Swanage was at least as busy at weekends as during the week, because of the extra holiday traffic. At times there were trains occupying both platforms, as on this occasion in 1960 when Class M7 No. 30111 is waiting to leave from the bay. The building to the right is the goods shed, which, in common with the station, engine shed and signal box, was built in the local Purbeck stone. The station buildings are in original condition except for the canopy, seen in the background, which was a Southern Railway replacement.

Plate 133 (right upper):   Main line trains were frequent visitors to Swanage, and in April 1960 a London-bound ramblers' excursion, hauled by 'West Country' class No. 34009 *Lyme Regis*, is seen through the road bridge at the station throat. The ground signal, on the far left of the picture, controls the exit from the engine shed. There were through coaches from Waterloo from several trains, including the 'Royal Wessex', and there were also complete through trains in the summer, some of which were routed via Ringwood. Even after the end of steam there was still one through train, consisting of a 'Bournemouth' trailer set and diesel locomotive, which was discontinued in 1969. The line was closed completely in 1972, but freight services were retained to Furzebrook, where an oil terminal has been built. Regular steam passenger trains now run again on the southern end of the line and the Swanage Railway Company hopes to run right through to Wareham in the future.

Plate 134 (right lower):   Seen on the main line passing Worgret Junction signal box is rebuilt 'Merchant Navy' class No. 35030 *Elder-Dempster Lines*, the last member of the class to be built. The train is the 10.30a.m. Waterloo to Weymouth service, on 11th April 1964. The crossover for the Swanage branch has now been taken out, and trains for Furzebrook work wrong line back to Wareham. Worgret Junction signal box has since been demolished.

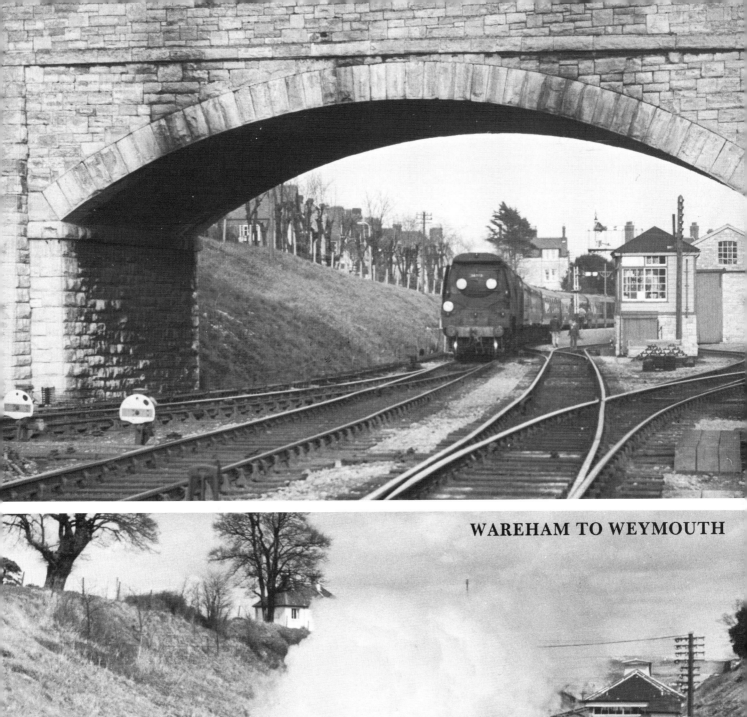

WAREHAM TO WEYMOUTH

Plate 135 (left upper): The 12.10p.m. Weymouth to Bournemouth Central train is pictured between Wool and Worgret Junction, headed by Standard Class 5MT, No. 73020, on 11th April 1964. The engine is fitted with a different style of tender to those on the engines of this class built for the Southern Region *(see Plates 4 & 20).* It was built for the Midland Region and when new, at the end of 1951, was allocated to Chester.

Plate 136 (left lower): A train for Waterloo enters Wool, behind rebuilt 'Merchant Navy' class, No. 35030 *Elder-Dempster Lines,* on 3rd June 1966. To the right, behind the 'up' platform, is a Pullman coach in use as a camping vehicle for holiday-makers. Wool is in an attractive part of Dorset and is the nearest station to Lulworth Cove, and the close proximity of army camps also enhanced both passenger and freight traffic at the station. From the 'up' line there was a short branch to Bovington Camp, which was exclusively for military traffic. This was opened in 1919, but closed nine years later. Wool station buildings were demolished a year after this photograph was taken and were replaced by functional, but unattractive, prefabricated units. The station was famous for having an LBSCR six-wheeled milk van on the 'down' side, which was grounded and used as a store. There was also the body of an SECR centre 'birdcage' passenger brake van nearby.

Plate 137 (above): A 'down' freight train waits in Dorchester yard, while Standard Class 4MT, No. 76005 leaves with an 'up' train to Bournemouth, on 3rd June 1966. The building behind the passenger train is the goods shed, and there was also a running shed, to the right beyond the photographer. This had an allocation of a few tank engines and small tender engines, mainly for local passenger train workings. The shed declined in importance once the Southern Region was able to use the GWR shed at Weymouth, and it eventually closed in 1957. On the 'down' side was the modern style signal box, which opened in 1959.

Plate 138: Dorchester South Station was probably unique in the British Isles, in that the 'up' platform was a terminus, whereas the 'down' platform was on the through line to Weymouth. All 'up' trains from Weymouth therefore had to reverse, in order to call at Dorchester. On 17th April 1956, 'West Country' class, No. 34105 *Swanage* backs its train, the 10.10a.m. 'all stations' from Weymouth to Bournemouth Central, into the 'up' platform. This odd layout arose because Dorchester was the terminus of the line from Southampton. Some years afterwards a second station, later called Dorchester West, was opened by the GWR on its line from Yeovil to Weymouth. The LSWR then built a connecting line to the GWR, to enable its trains to run on to Weymouth, and a 'down' platform was subsequently installed on this line. No corresponding 'up' platform was built, and the terminus platform continued to be used until 1970.

Plate 139: Class Q No. 30536 is seen outside the shed on 17th April 1956.

Plate 140: The railway and main road follow each other between Dorchester and Weymouth, and at Upwey the road crosses the railway on a hairpin hill. Here the railway enters a tunnel, followed by the road overbridge. At this point, in early June 1966, Class 5MT No. 73022 is seen with the 4.50p.m. Weymouth to Bournemouth stopping train.

Plate 141: 'Battle of Britain' class No. 34071 *601 Squadron* passes Upwey Wishing Well Halt on the 3.50p.m. Weymouth to Waterloo train on 3rd June 1966. Only minor trains stopped here and it was closed in 1957.

Plate 142: Upwey was an excellent place from which to watch the heavy trains struggling up the long climb out of Weymouth, which, at its steepest, was 1 in 50. The platforms were still in place at the time this photograph was taken. 'Battle of Britain' class No. 34086 *219 Squadron* makes disappointingly easy work of hauling the six coaches forming the 5.35p.m. Weymouth to Waterloo train, on a dry and clear summer evening in 1966.

WEYMOUTH RUNNING SHED

Plate 143 (left upper):   The far roads of engine sheds often contained interesting vehicles, in this instance an SR Ironclad corridor coach for use in the Weymouth breakdown train. It is numbered DS 70123 and was formerly TK No 753.

Plate 144 (left lower):   Although the LSWR had a small shed at Weymouth, this was out of use by 1939, after which the Southern used the much larger GWR premises. With regional boundary changes in February 1958, the shed was administered by the Southern Region and was given the code 71G. On shed in June 1966 are several Bulleid Pacifics and BR Standard tender engines. In the foreground is Class 4MT No. 76006 and behind this is rebuilt 'Merchant Navy' Pacific No. 35007 *Aberdeen Commonwealth.*

Plate 145 (above):   With their backs to the wall and fighting for survival, in the last days of steam on the Southern are 'Battle of Britain' class locomotives No. 34071 *601 Squadron* in rebuilt condition, and unrebuilt Pacific No. 34086 *219 Squadron.*

Plate 146: Two Pacifics ready to work evening trains to London in the summer of 1966.

Tailpiece: The memorable sight of one of the Southern Railway's powerful Class S15 locomotives No. 30833 heading west towards Southampton five years before the end of steam.

INDEX OF LOCATIONS